Little People, BIG DREAMS®
BEATRIX POTTER

Written by
Maria Isabel Sánchez Vegara

Illustrated by
Sara Rhys

Frances Lincoln
Children's Books

In a lovely part of London called South Kensington, there lived a very curious child. Her parents named her Helen, but she became known by her middle name: Beatrix. She felt a deep love for animals, trees and everything in nature.

Beatrix didn't go to school. She learned at home with a teacher, and her only friends were her little brother, Bertram, and their many pets. They had mice, fluffy rabbits, bats and even a prickly hedgehog! She loved drawing them all.

Her parents soon noticed Beatrix had an irresistible desire to draw everything, from the birds in a book to the insects she saw at the Natural History Museum.

She also kept a diary. It was written in a secret code only she could understand.

Each summer, Beatrix spent her holidays in the countryside in Scotland, and later in England's Lake District — a place so beautiful, it looked like it came straight out of a story book. Beatrix hoped it would stay that way forever . . .

After years of art lessons, Beatrix started earning a little money with her drawings. Some became Christmas cards, and others were used in books of poems and stories. She dreamt that one day, she'd make a book of her own.

Then, while on holiday, Beatrix sent a letter to her little friend Noel. In it, she wrote and drew a made-up story about her rabbit, Peter. It was funny and just a tiny bit scary. Noel loved it so much that Beatrix decided to turn it into a book.

The Tale of Peter Rabbit followed a naughty little rabbit who sneaked into Mr McGregor's garden after his mother told him not to. Beatrix made him feel so real that he leapt off the page, right into everyone's hearts!

She believed in her story so much that she paid for it to be printed. People loved it! The next year, a company offered to publish it for her and printed many more copies. That was the start of her life as a children's writer and illustrator.

Beatrix had another great idea — what if kids could play with Peter Rabbit, not just read about him? She made a doll that looked like him. She also created games, wallpaper and tea sets using her book characters, in a way that was totally new.

She used the money she made to buy a farm in the Lake District. Later, Beatrix married William, a kind man who also loved nature.

Together, they worked on the land and helped protect the hills, fields and sheep around them.

Yet she never stopped writing! Beatrix made more than twenty books filled with exciting adventures, beautiful drawings and unforgettable characters. Later, her stories even came to life in cartoons and films.

She gave much of her land and farms to the National Trust, a group that takes care of special places in the United Kingdom. Thanks to her, the countryside that inspired her stories has been kept safe for everyone to enjoy.

And still today, little Beatrix and all her furry, feathery and froggy friends bring joy to children everywhere, reminding us that even the smallest creatures have a story to tell.

BEATRIX POTTER

(Born 1866 – Died 1943)

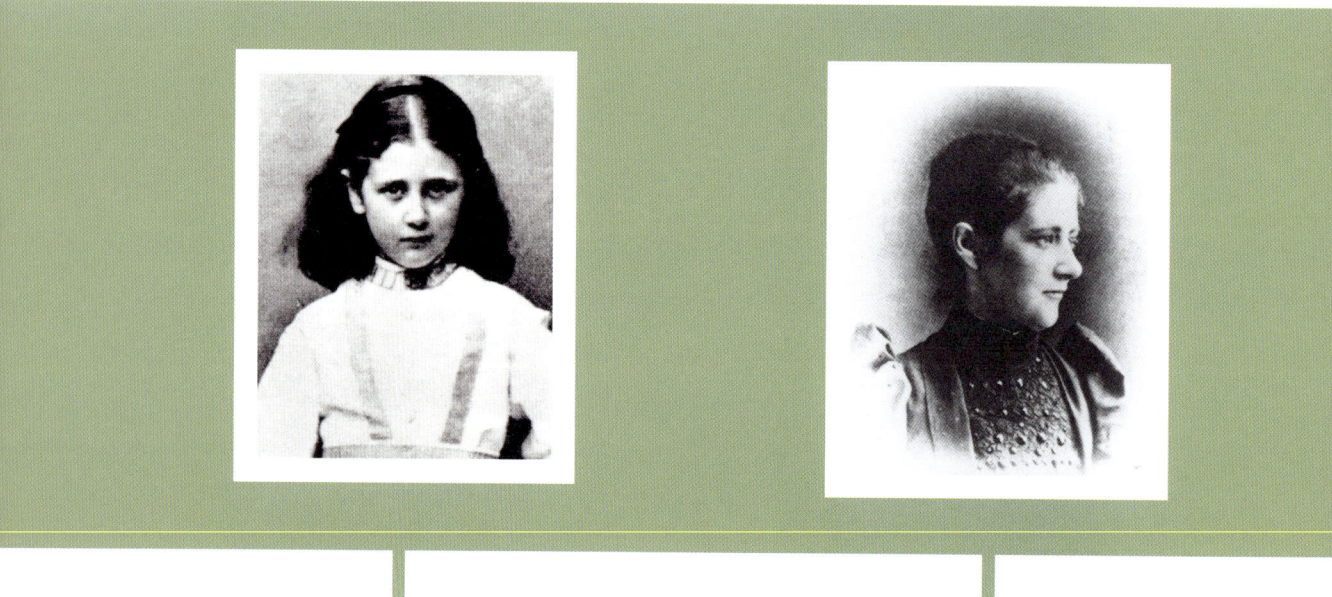

c. 1870s

1889

Helen Beatrix Potter grew up in London in a wealthy, artistic Victorian family. She was taught at home, and spent a lot of time reading and drawing. During long summer holidays, Beatrix and her brother, Bertram, roamed the countryside, collecting frogs, lizards, mice and other creatures to sketch. Some were even smuggled home as pets! As an adult, Beatrix began selling her illustrations. She spent hours at London's Natural History Museum, studying and sketching plants and insects, and even went on to write a scientific paper about fungi. When she was twenty-seven, she sent a story based on her real-life pet rabbit, Peter Piper, to cheer up the unwell son of a friend. In other letters, she wrote stories about a fishing frog and a rude squirrel called Nutkin. Years later, Beatrix decided to turn

c. 1890s   c. 1900s

the story of Peter the rabbit into a little book and paid for a small number of copies to be made. *The Tale of Peter Rabbit* became so popular that many more were printed, and it went on to become one of the most loved children's stories of all time. Beatrix wrote another twenty-two tales, some based on her actual pets, including a bunny called Benjamin and a hedgehog named Mrs Tiggy-Winkle. In 1905, she bought Hill Top, a farm in the Lake District. She married a man named William Heelis and threw herself into farming and raising sheep. After her death in 1943, she gave fifteen farms and over 4,000 acres of land to the conservation charity the National Trust, in the hope that the beautiful countryside she loved would remain protected.

Want to find out more about **Beatrix Potter**?

Have a read of this great book:

V&A Introduces: Beatrix Potter

If you're in the UK, you can visit Hill Top,
which is protected by the National Trust.

To dear Delilah, dream big. The world awaits!

Text © 2026 Maria Isabel Sánchez Vegara. Illustrations © 2026 Sara Rhys
Original idea of the series by Maria Isabel Sánchez Vegara, published by Alba Editorial, s.l.u.
"Little People, BIG DREAMS" and "Pequeña & Grande" are trademarks of
Alba Editorial s.l.u. and/or Beautifool Couple S.L.
First published in the UK in 2026 by Frances Lincoln Children's Books, an imprint of The Quarto Group.
1 Triptych Place, London, SE1 9SH, United Kingdom. T 020 7700 6700 www.Quarto.com
EEA Representation, WTS Tax d.o.o., Žanova ulica 3, 4000 Kranj, Slovenia. www.wts-tax.si

All rights reserved.
No part of this publication may be reproduced, stored in a retrieval system, or transmitted, in any form,
or by any means, electrical, mechanical, photocopying, recording or otherwise without the prior written
permission of the publisher or a licence permitting restricted copying.

This book is not authorised, licensed or approved by the estate of Beatrix Potter.
Any faults are the publisher's who will be happy to rectify for future printings.
A catalogue record for this book is available from the British Library.
ISBN 978-1-80570-162-0
Set in Futura BT.

Published by Juliet Matthews · Edited by Lucy Menzies
Editorial management by Izzie Hewitt
Designed by Sasha Moxon, Izzy Bowman and Karissa Santos
Production by Robin Boothroyd
Manufactured in Shanghai, China CC102025
1 3 5 7 9 8 6 4 2

Photographic acknowledgements (pages 28-29, from left to right): 1. An undated library file picture of a young Beatrix Potter, aged nine. 2. 1889: English writer Beatrix Potter. (Photo by Hulton Archive/Getty Images) 3. Portrait of British children's author Beatrix Potter, 1890s. (Photo by Express Newspapers/Getty Images) 4. Beatrix Potter by King – Image ID: JW69J6 (RM).

Collect the Little People, BIG DREAMS® series:

FRIDA KAHLO	COCO CHANEL	MAYA ANGELOU	AMELIA EARHART	AGATHA CHRISTIE	MARIE CURIE	ROSA PARKS	AUDREY HEPBURN	EMMELINE PANKHURST
ELLA FITZGERALD	ADA LOVELACE	JANE AUSTEN	GEORGIA O'KEEFFE	HARRIET TUBMAN	ANNE FRANK	MOTHER TERESA	JOSEPHINE BAKER	L. M. MONTGOMERY
JANE GOODALL	SIMONE DE BEAUVOIR	MUHAMMAD ALI	STEPHEN HAWKING	MARIA MONTESSORI	VIVIENNE WESTWOOD	MAHATMA GANDHI	DAVID BOWIE	WILMA RUDOLPH
DOLLY PARTON	BRUCE LEE	RUDOLF NUREYEV	ZAHA HADID	MARY SHELLEY	MARTIN LUTHER KING JR.	DAVID ATTENBOROUGH	ASTRID LINDGREN	EVONNE GOOLAGONG
BOB DYLAN	ALAN TURING	BILLIE JEAN KING	GRETA THUNBERG	JESSE OWENS	JEAN-MICHEL BASQUIAT	ARETHA FRANKLIN	CORAZON AQUINO	PELÉ
ERNEST SHACKLETON	STEVE JOBS	AYRTON SENNA	LOUISE BOURGEOIS	ELTON JOHN	JOHN LENNON	PRINCE	CHARLES DARWIN	CAPTAIN TOM MOORE
HANS CHRISTIAN ANDERSEN	STEVIE WONDER	MEGAN RAPINOE	MARY ANNING	MALALA YOUSAFZAI	ANDY WARHOL	RUPAUL	MICHELLE OBAMA	MINDY KALING

| IRIS APFEL | ROSALIND FRANKLIN | RUTH BADER GINSBURG | MARILYN MONROE | KAMALA HARRIS | ALBERT EINSTEIN | CHARLES DICKENS | YOKO ONO | MICHAEL JORDAN |

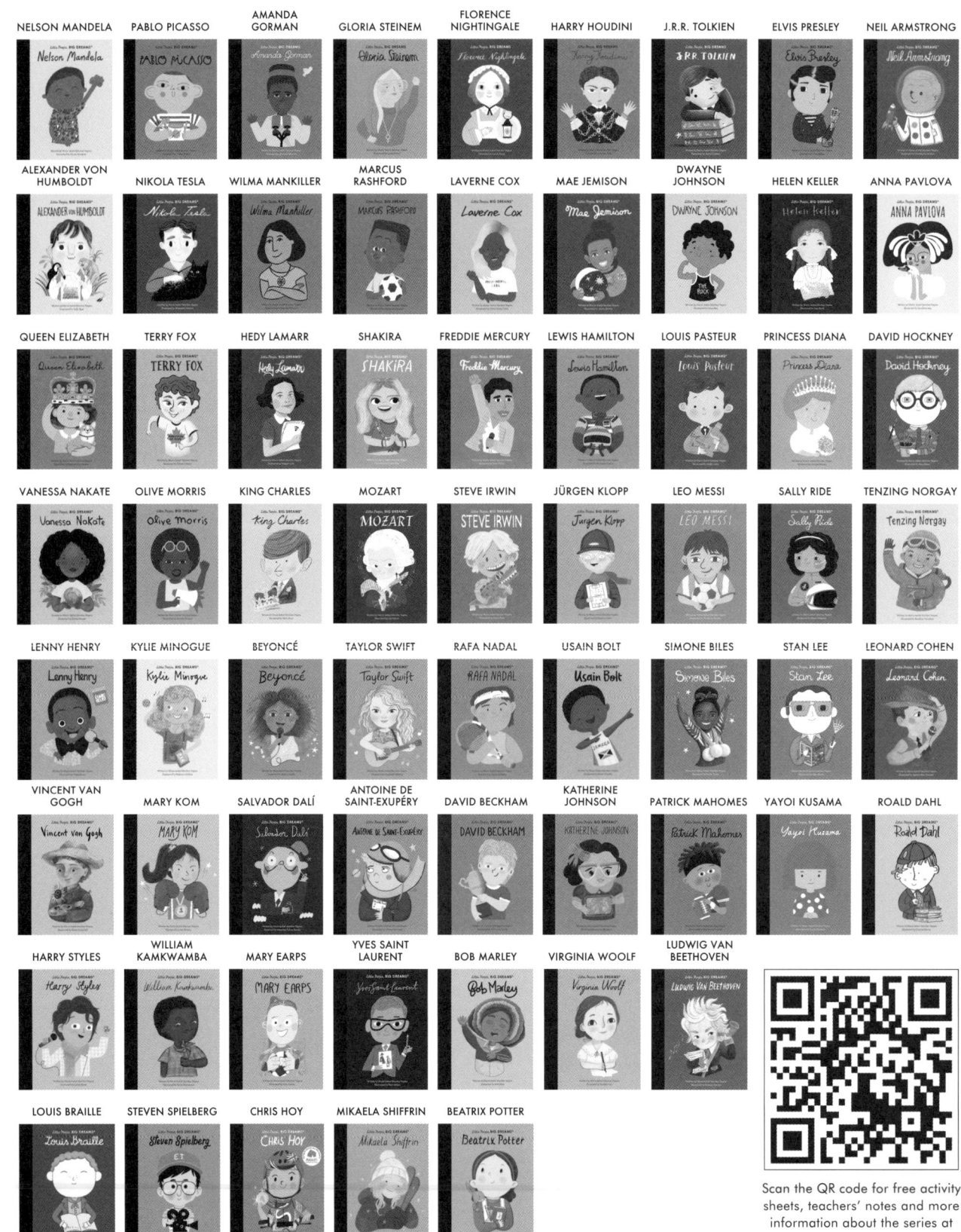